I Challenge You...
I Promise You...

1 Challenge You...
1 Promise You...

VOLUME II

PAUL H. DUNN

Bookcraft
Salt Lake City, Utah

Library of Congress Catalog Card Number: 72-90323

ISBN 0-88494-400-X

2nd Printing, 1980

Lithographed in the United States of America
PUBLISHERS PRESS
Salt Lake City, Utah

I Challenge You...
I Promise You...

VOLUME II

PAUL H. DUNN

Bookcraft

Salt Lake City, Utah

2nd Printing, 1980

Lithographed in the United States of America
PUBLISHERS PRESS
Salt Lake City, Utah

THE PROMISES

ACKNOWLEDGMENTS

Eight years ago,
in a hotel room overlooking New York's LaGuardia Airport,
Richard Eyre and I put our heads together and finished
the last chapter of *I Challenge You, I Promise You.*

Since that day we have kept a file
of other challenges, other promises.
Since that day we have marked our scriptures
according to their challenges and connected promises.
Since that day we have come to *think* in terms
of challenges and promises — to believe,
as the scripture says, that blessings
are predicated, are dependent on,
particular principles. Even more than that,
we've come to accept the thrilling truth that *any* blessing
can be obtained by finding and keeping the principle
or principles upon which it is predicated.

There is a total, unchanging justice in the universe.
Challenges and promises
are the "cause" and "effect" parts of laws —
laws that God Himself both operates and observes.

Emerson said it in these words:

> "Cause and effect are two sides of one fact. Every
> secret is told, every crime is punished, every virtue
> is rewarded, every wrong is redressed, in silence and
> certainty . . . cause and effect, means and ends, seed and
> fruit, cannot be severed; for the effect already blooms
> in the cause, the end pre-exists in the means, the
> fruit in the seed."

Indeed, the promise preexists in the challenge.

I am grateful that we live in a world
that works this way.
I am grateful to my wife, Jeanne, and to Linda Eyre,
both of whom so often understand more of what is said than
    done.
I express special thanks to Sharene Hansen
for her secretarial assistance.
I am grateful to Richard Eyre for the opportunity
of working and thinking with him.
My collaboration with Richard Eyre extends
back over many years and some six books. The first
I Challenge You, I Promise You, volume one,
started ten years ago in Boston when I was mission president
and Richard was a graduate student at Harvard University.

The idea for the second volume of *I Challenge You, I
    Promise You*
began when Richard was a mission president
and I was touring his mission.

He and I have exchanged ideas too on books which bear
only his name or mine — for example,
on his *Discovery of Joy* and *What Manner of Man*,
as well as others he has written but not yet published.
We expect to continue this pleasant and fruitful
relation of collaboration and exchange of ideas
in forthcoming publications.

That file I mentioned — the one dealing with other challenges
    and promises —
is bulging now.
It's time to start another book.

THE CHALLENGES

8

PREFACE: I Challenge You to Accept Christ's Three Great Invitations of Mortality

Clearly,
without room for slippage or misinterpretation,
He tells us,
"I, the Lord, am bound when ye do what I say." (D&C 82:10.)
Do we grasp that?
Laws! Cause and effect! If you *do* this, you *will* receive that!
Could He make it clearer?
Perhaps so:
"There is a law,
irrevocably
decreed in heaven before the foundations of this world,
upon which
all
blessings are predicated.
And when we obtain
any
blessing from God, it is by obedience to
that law
upon which it is predicated." (D&C 130:20-21; italics added.)

God our Father has much (all) that He wants to give us.
But He works by natural law
and must give by natural law.

Thus He made this space-lab earth and designed into it
the laws that, if kept, allow us to receive
the gifts He wants to give.

His greatest gifts for us are:
1. Peace.
2. Eternal joy.
3. A kingdom of our own.

He has extended to us three great invitations
that lead respectively to these three great gifts:
1. To come to know Him (peace).
2. To find the true joys of mortality (eternal joy).
3. To begin righteous families (kingdoms).

These are His invitations.
They lead to promises that only He can make.

I challenge you to accept those invitations.
I challenge you to accept the challenges
that *enable* you to accept His invitations;
and as you do,

SECTION I: He Invites You to Come
to Know Him (Jesus Christ)

The purpose of eternal life is to know Christ (John 17:3).
Knowing Christ *is* knowing the gospel;
it is knowing perfection,
knowing our ultimate goal.

We are here on earth to experience directions
that can expand us
to the capacity necessary to begin knowing Him.

Knowing Him is not only the purpose of life,
it is the reward of life.

He tells us to work out our salvation
(which means knowing Him).
He tells us to love Him and to love all men
(which means knowing Him).
He tells us to be perfect
(which means knowing Him).

He invites us to know Him;
and as we do,

98

11

. . . *His peace.*

SECTION III: He Promises Us Peace

**I Challenge You to Learn to Ask Yourself,
"What Would He Do?"**

Because of His perfect knowledge,
Christ is able to predict what we will do.
Also, because of His perfection,
we can become able to predict what He would do.
Knowing this, and patterning our lives as close to His life as
    we can,
is the key to all right decisions, to all right behavior,
to peace in the world, to peace within self.

I challenge you to form the habit of asking that question.
Asking it is the ultimate application of the "as if" principle
(which teaches that acting *as if* we are something
is the surest way to *become* that something).

I challenge you to ask the question
whenever you face a decision.
Countless times each day we subconsciously ask ourselves,
"What should I do?" We ask it from the moment we wake
until the moment we sleep. We ask it, in some form,
before we do anything that we do.
But there is a *better* question to ask:
"What would *He* do?"
In a way it is the same question,
because what He would do and what we should do
are always the same.

But it is better to ask it the second way because,
in doing so,
we come to know Him better
and we are prompted to find out the things about Him
that we don't know.
And in asking the question the second way,
we know we *can* do what we should do—
because He did.

I challenge you to ask that second question at *all* moments—
even when you do not face a decision.
Ask it while you are commuting to work.
Ask it while you are watching your children.
Ask it while you are attending a party.
In the question you will find ways to make others happy,
ways to help those who are in need,
ways to get more out of (and put more into)
the ordinary experiences of life.

You will normally know the answer the moment you
ask the question.
The light of Christ (which is in all men) often supplies us the
        answer
(but *not* until we ask the question).

I challenge you to form the habit of asking the question,
because asking is very nearly the same as doing.
(Once you have asked yourself what He would do,
it's rather hard to do something He would not do—
much harder, at least, than if you had not asked
the question.)

I Promise You the Peace of Beginning to Know Him

I promise you that as you ask yourself what He would do,
you will think more about Him.
And as you think more about Him
you will know Him better and you will be more aware of Him.
And as you become more aware of Him, you will ask for His
                help more.
And as you ask more, you will receive more.

83

I challenge you to ask the question;
and as you do,

I Challenge You to Study His Life Enough to Know "What He Would Do"

We ask, "What should I do?"
He answers, "Do what I would do!"
We ask, "What is that?"
He answers, "You should know!"

This is the essence of many of our prayers.
I challenge you to become an avid student of the most
       important
subject of all: our Elder Brother, Jesus Christ.

The textbook is the scriptures,
four standard works that
are set up to provide a series of clues,
insights, and flashes of light
as to who and what Jesus Christ really is, as to
what He would do in your situation, as to
what *you* should do to be like Him.

I challenge you to search the scriptures daily (Acts 17:11),
to ponder and delight in the scriptures (2 Nephi 4:15),
to know God's will through them (Alma 17:2),
to know through them that Jesus is the Christ (Acts 18:28).

Question: How?
How to really get into them, how to be interested,
how to understand?
Is there a system? a particular method?
I asked that question to an old and wise man once,

and he said,
"I can give you a system for eating,
but it is much better to simply be hungry!"

So how does one get hungry for the scriptures?
Well, this challenge and the incredible promises that
go with it
may whet your appetite; but there are two other keys:

First: I challenge you to
learn and profit by likening all scriptures
to your own situation (1 Nephi 19:23),
(or by likening yourself to the time and place
of the scripture).
Either move yourself back
(Like time traveling; open the book and *be* there—
actually imagine yourself *there*, like a mouse in the corner,
invisible to those you are watching and listening to),
or move the scripture forward
(imagine the words being said to you, now, or to
someone you know today; think of a similar situation
today, and "retranslate" what you read into the present).

Second: I challenge you to
make effective notes in the margins of your scriptures.
With a fine-point pen, write your thoughts,
your conclusions,
and the ideas the scriptures bring to your mind.
The next time you read that page of scripture
you will also read those marginal notes.
Your own thoughts will return to you as old friends.

You will feel that you are in a familiar place.
You will find that you can remember your own words
better than anyone else's.
Make margin notes about how the scripture applies to *today*,
and about how you would feel if you'd been *there* then,
and, most of all, about Christ — His personality, His
    temperament, His perfection.

I challenge you
to divide and analyze His word (2 Timothy 2:15), and to put
        your
conclusions into margin notes.

I challenge you to hunger and thirst for the scriptures;
to study Jesus Christ;
to become a student-disciple of all He did and all He said,
both directly and through His prophets;
and as you do,

I Promise You the Peace of Knowing What He Would Do

*I promise you
the peace of being able to answer the original question —
That you will know what Christ would do,
and thus be able to pattern your life after His.
I promise you, further,
that you will find prosperity and success (Joshua 1:8);
that you will find wisdom (2 Timothy 3:15)
and comfort and hope (Romans 15:4);
that in a world of fallacy and deceit,
you will not be deceived (Joseph Smith 1:37);
that your mind will be quickened (Psalm 119:50 and D&C
33:16);
and that you will find salvation (D&C 68:4) and eternal life
(John 5:39).*

**I Challenge You to Discover That Faith Is
Even More Valuable Than Self-Confidence**

"I, myself, can do anything" — part false, part true.
"I, myself, can do nothing" — part true, part false.
"I, with God's blessing and help, can do anything" — true.

Focus on the part false / part true statement.
Self-confidence is a valuable thing, but it is partially based
on a false premise;
for, in fact, we can do little without the light of Christ,
we can do little good without the Spirit.

Even for people who don't know this,
self-confidence has a way of
"running out."
Can you identify with the common experience of
facing a tough challenge — of saying to yourself,
"I can do it,"
and hearing your faint, but powerful, subconscious voice say,
"No you can't, you never have; when the chips are down,
you'll blow it"?

Now focus on the other two statements.
Together, they simply say,
"God is the source of *all* power. With His power,
anything can be done. Without it, not much."

Thus the truly powerful man does not say,
"*I* can do it";
he says,
"I *can* do it, but with God's help."

The difference in those two statements is enormous.
The first puts anxiety, strain, weight
on the speaker.
The second brings peace, strength, commitment to
God and to His laws
(by which all things can be done).

As an example, imagine the difference between two
                    quarterbacks.
One calls his own plays.
His self-confidence gets him through on some,
but gets him sacked on others.
The other quarterback has a radio receiver in his helmet.
His plays are called by an infallible coach
who sits high in the press box.
Instead of partial self-confidence
(and *self*-confidence can never be more than partial),
the second quarterback has total assurance
that every play is right.

We are all "wired" to God through the light of Christ.
Still, the analogy is not strong enough;
for, in life, faith can give us not only access to the right plays,
but the power needed to execute them.

We know how to operate some laws
(the law of muscular force can pick up a pencil
and overcome gravity).
God knows how to operate *all* law—
and our faith can be the agent that substitutes His knowledge
for our lack of it.
(Peter's knowledge couldn't operate the law of levitation, but
        his faith activated Christ's knowledge, *which could*.
Thus Peter walked on water.)

I challenge you to lean *off* of your own understanding,
to *exercise* faith
(Joseph Smith said faith works by mental effort),
to carefully think through what you want;
then to ask God's confirmation of your goals,
then to readjust until confirmation comes,
then to ask for help in knowing how to achieve your goals,
then to express love for God and faith in His power,
then to ask for help in doing what you've planned.

I Promise You the Peace of a Calm, Inner Power

. . . which will cast out fear.
I promise you
a solid, total assurance
that what you are leaning on
is not the straw house of your own feeble ability,
but the brick and mortar
of God's total knowledge
and total love.

More than any other scriptural admonition,
God asks us to ask.
I challenge you to do so, thus upgrading
any self-confidence you have into faith;
and as you do,

I Challenge You to Turn Prayer into a Dialogue

"All you had to do was ask."
A common phrase among men, in situations where
an opportunity has just been lost.

Perhaps it will also be a common phrase
from God to man
in the next world:
"All you had to do was ask — and listen.
I would have told you what to do,
how to be happy,
what values to embrace,
what decisions to make."

In basketball, the ultimate defense is keeping the other team's
      man
from getting the ball.
Without the ball he can never score.
Once he gets it, you resort to the next-best defense:
keeping him from doing anything effective with it.
Satan's ultimate defense is keeping us
from getting God's Spirit and inspiration.
He succeeds if he can do one of two things —
if he can keep us from asking, or if he can keep us from
      listening.
Failing those, his next-best defense is
keeping us from doing anything effective
with God's inspiration.

I challenge you to ask,
to ask thoughtfully and clearly and earnestly.
And I challenge you to listen
intently, with the commitment to act on answers.

If you had an advice appointment with a
wise and powerful man,
you would want to be careful
1. to show proper respect and gratitude,
2. to ask him the right questions,
3. to remember his answers.
Notes would help you do all three.

I challenge you to use notes to improve
your interviews with God;
to have a deep, sweet prayer at least once each day
(Mosiah 4:11),
prepared for by notes

on what you wish to express thanks for
and what you wish to ask for.

I challenge you to pause often in prayer, to listen,
and to take notes on the feelings you experience.
I challenge you to find a peaceful place and time
for this divine dialogue,
and I suggest that you choose the fresh and early
over the tired and late.

I challenge you to keep these notes in your journal
and to review and ponder them often,
seeing their fulfillment,
noting your progress.

I challenge you to stay on your knees long enough
to feel the connection complete,
to hear with your heart the end of circuit-busy buzzing
and the light-clear channel of contact established.

I challenge you to persist in this kind of prayer
day after day,
giving it high enough priority that it is not left out
when other demands invade your life.

I challenge you to turn prayer
into thoughtful, soul-expanding dialogue;
and as you do,

I Promise You the Peace of Listening to God

*I promise you the peace of feeling that
your ears-to-God work as well as your voice-to-God.
I promise you that you will carry away from prayer
specific instruction
from the Master Planner of the universe.
I promise you that He will teach you to pray as you pray;
that prayer will become so sweet, so delicious, that
you will be slow to rise to your knees
and anxious to go to them again.*

I Challenge You to Be "Rebaptized" Each Week
Through the Sacrament

By nature, there are two things that men need
continually.
One is repentance (for we are never perfect);
the other is recommitment (so that commitments
strengthen rather than weaken with the passage of time).

God, in His perfect wisdom, gives us a beautiful means of
repetition
in connection with both needs.
The means is called the sacrament.

The sacrament is (should be) a time of repentance and
      recommitment.
In order to be effective,
it must be prepared for.
When it is prepared for, the sacrament can be a time for
self-examination,
expanded understanding,
and the enhancement of faith —
a cleansing joy!

I challenge you to do precisely what we are told
in scripture
and in the sacramental prayers themselves.
Before you go to church (preferably early on Sunday morning):

1. Examine yourself (1 Corinthians 11:28).
Look to your goals, your plans, your patriarchal blessing;
examine your progress;
set new objectives and self-commitments.
2. Evaluate yourself in terms of the commandments (D&C 20:77).
Look for any unrighteousness (whether of commission or omission),
and ask for forgiveness and commit to change.
3. Remember Him (D&C 20:79).
Meditate or study about the Savior
until some new quality, some new facet of His
life or personality or power,
occurs to your mind.
During the sacrament:
1. Review in your mind your morning conclusions concerning your
objectives and your repentance,
and how both are dependent on the Atonement and the Light of Christ.
2. Consciously take upon yourself Christ's name (D&C 20:77),
remembering your new thought about His nature,
covenanting to try to be like Him in that respect.
3. Pray.
Thank the Father for the Son,
for His life for us and His death for us.

Ask the Father to help His weak son or weak daughter
become more like His strong son. Say, with David of old,
"Create in me a clean heart, O God; and renew a right spirit
     within me." (Psalm 51:10.)

I challenge you to put forth the effort
to do all of this
each Sunday,
to thus renew the covenants of baptism
(and thus be "rebaptized");
and as you do,

I Promise You the Peace of the Sacrament Prayers' Promise

*. . . the great and simple promise that
you will have His Spirit to be with you,
that you will feel His light as you partake,
and that you will have
eternal life (John 6:51, 3 Nephi 20:8).*

I Challenge You to Understand How to Both Love and Fear Christ

Among men,
those we fear are hard to love, and
those we love are hard to fear.
Yet these terms are not opposites
(control is opposite of fear; hate, of love).
So perhaps it is possible to both love and fear.
A child, particularly after making some mistake,
could both love and fear his father;
and, had the child a good father,
the fear would *relate* to the love — it would be a fear
of disappointing, of letting down, of not measuring up to
the expectations of one so loved and so loving.

This kind of love- and respect-related fear
becomes even clearer
to those who have stood and talked eye to eye
with a prophet.
Love wells up and abounds,
but it is somehow interlaced with the fear of
being with a man who can see
through you — into you.

The motivation of fear without love is negative
and robs man of freedom, of initiative, of nobility.
The motivation of love so profound that it includes
respect, humility, and *fear* is positive, purposeful—
even thrilling.
The first is the fear of punishment, fear which is not of God
      (2 Timothy 1:7).
The second is the fear of God, which brings mercy (Luke 1:50).
The first is taught by the precept of man (Isaiah 29:13),
and is due to wickedness (Alma 36:7).
The second is taught by the Spirit of God (Ecclesiastes 12:13),
and brings happiness and joy (Psalm 128:1-6).

Fear, even in ordinary, daily terms,
piques our senses, speeds our pulse, gives us insight.
Righteous fear of God
piques our spiritual sense, prompts our repentance,
brings us closer to Him.

89

29

It was both love and fear that raised Abraham's knife
over his son Isaac.
Paul and Alma the Younger each felt both fear and love
after their forceful conversions.
Every man, struggling both to comprehend
and to please God,
feels both.

The Lord, in His earthly ministry,
replaced Old Testament fear with New Testament love.
Still, there is evidence that His apostles deeply feared Him;
and that as their love grew, so did their fear.
Fear of God actually *overcomes* the fear of man.
(One who fears God, automatically becomes unafraid
of men's pressure on him to break a commandment of God.)

Fear of a man would lead us away from that man.
Fear-love of God draws us to Him,
and causes us to look forward to His coming (D&C 45:39).

The imperfect must always fear the perfect;
love-fear is imperfect man's love for perfect God.
It is only when our love and our lives become perfect
that all fear will be gone.
(Perfect love casteth out *all* fear; 1 John 4:18.)

I challenge you to understand and respect God
enough to find true humility,
enough to find true love,
enough to find true fear.

I challenge you to comprehend
that He made you,
that He owns you,
that His light sustains you.

I challenge you to love and fear Him enough
that you cannot do either of the two things that offend Him
      (D&C 59:21):
1. Fail to acknowledge His hand in all things.
2. Obey not His commandments.

I challenge you to fear Him with all your soul;
I challenge you to love Him with all your life;
and as you do,

I Promise You the Peace of Having No Other Fears

I promise you
that your capacity to love Christ's other children will expand,
that your progress and growth toward Him
will have Godspeed.

I Challenge You to Give Yourself to Him

C. S. Lewis, in a fable for children,
writes of a horse named Huin who, at a particular point,
is overpowered by a profound mixture of
love, fear, respect, humility, and joy
for Aslan (the lion — a God-Savior figure).
At that moment,
Huin's feeling is so deep that she can only say
that she desires to be eaten by Aslan —
that she would rather be eaten by Him
than to herself eat anyone or anything else.

The ultimate desire of the deepest love
is to want to be absorbed by,
to be a part of,
to give self to.

Indeed, this is the way the Savior loved us.
He absorbed Himself into our imperfect world.
He became a part of all He met.
He gave Himself to us and for us,
and He said,
"A new commandment I give unto you,
That ye love one another, as I have loved you." (John 13:34.)
To love one another was not a new commandment.

But
to love each other (and Him)
as He had loved us
(totally, selflessly)
was new, and will always be new.

How, then, do we give ourselves to Him?
What do we give?
Our time, our talents, our ambitions,
our possessions, our energies,
our minds,
our hearts!
Who do we give them to?
To Christ!
To His way of life!
To His commandments!
To *everything* He asked us to do!

We do this
by asking what He would do, and doing it;
by studying and loving His life;
by developing faith;
by "sweet prayer";
by taking upon us His name each week;
by loving and fearing Him.

The marvel is that Christ *already* owns us —
first, because He made us,

second, because He purchased us with His atonement —
yet He gives us free agency, and
the chance to give ourselves
to Him.

I challenge you to give yourself to Christ;
and as you do,

I Promise You the Peace of Knowing That
All He Has Is Yours

SECTION II: He Invites You to Seek and Find Mortality's Joys

This earth,
and our mortal existence upon it,
is our springboard into eternity.

The earth's purpose is to serve as a great teacher,
to present us with physical test patterns
of spiritual realities.

Here we taste
marriage and parenthood, agency and decision,
act and consequence, reach and fulfillment,
search and light, law and promise.

Here, in the arena of opposing forces and new responsibility,
we first sense the expanding joy
of agency used, commitments made.

Here, the Lord and Savior invites us
to have joy (2 Nephi 2:25),
to discover and experience the joys of
obedience,
of sacrifice, of service, of stewardship;
and as we do,

I Challenge You to Find the Full Joy of the Physical Earth and Your Physical Body

A hot shower on a cold winter day,
the first bite of food after a long fast,
the refreshment of sleep, the stretch of exercise,
the glory of a sunset,
the peace of a forest.

The simple joys of natural and physical things
spread like a blanket across our lives, and there are
moments when we marvel
at both the beauty
and the intricacy of the eye's incredible camera,
the heart's incredible pump —
at the gentle change of seasons,
the desert evening's stars.

We walk through mortality surrounded by wonder.
Why is it, then, that so often it takes
a poet's words,
or a child's awe,
or a rare moment of welling emotion,
or even crisis and loss (or near loss) of some of the beauty
before we really notice it —
before we truly appreciate our incredible earth, our incredible
        bodies?

Two children's stories make the point.
The first is about Ernie, who is picked up by a spaceship.
Ernie visits the world of Thoyd, which is made of
flat purple plastic because its people had to construct it
when their first world got too dirty, too polluted to live on.
Thoyd is great for roller skating, but bad for everything else —
there is no nature, no beauty, no variety.
Ernie goes back to earth and *sees* the sunsets,
smells the flowers, *hears* the birds —
loves and cares for the earth.

The second story is of Ben, who goes to seek riches
by asking the land's four rich men how to acquire wealth.
The first, old and stooped, tells Ben he is rich because
he has strong legs;
the second, dim-eyed from years at his ledger books,
tells Ben he is rich because he has clear vision;
and so on.

Do we have to be an Ernie or a Ben to gain the full joy
of physical mortality?
Yes,
in the sense that we must appreciate
and be more widely aware.

I challenge you to tune your senses,
to observe, to notice, to pause and appreciate.

I challenge you to spend fifteen consecutive minutes
in "gratitude prayer," a prayer in which you do nothing but
        thank the Lord
for every physical blessing of the earth and of your body.

I challenge you to use your body more—
to run, to exercise regularly,
to remember that one key difference between man-made things
and God-made things
is that use *wears out* the first and *strengthens* the second.

I challenge you to bridle your appetites (Alma 38:12)—
to not eat too much; to not sleep too much;
to not buy too much;
to discipline yourself; to keep your life simple;
to appreciate each thing, each place, each idea.

I challenge you to remember
that you
shouted for joy (Job 38:7) when first you were told
of your chance to experience this physical existence.
I challenge you to find the joy within it,
the joy that men are made mortal to receive (2 Nephi 2:25).

I challenge you to turn all that you see,
all that you feel,
into joy;
and as you do,

I Promise You Physical Joys That "Carry Over" into Eternity

. . . that what you learn to use and appreciate here
will still be appreciated there.
I promise you physical, temporal joy.
I promise you that each day will hold excitement
and happy surprise.

I Challenge You to Find the Full Joy of Relationships and Achievements

"Eternal progression" —
the commanding term echoes through the very columns
of the restored gospel.
It stands strong as the hallmark of our lifestyle as well as of
      our faith.
It is opposite the traditional objective of "eternal rest."

The blessing of standing on the side of eternal progression
is that true progress always yields true joy.

Progression "happens" in two essential ways.
One way is through achievements, wherein we
do, or learn, or gain.
The other way is through relationships, wherein we
expand or give.
Both ways produce joy —
partly because they ripple outward, into other lives,
and are reflected back into our own,
and partly because they each are progress,
and progress and joy always link.

Also, relationships and achievements produce joy because
they are exciting; in fact, *exciting* could be defined
as "a new achievement or a new relationship."

Every person is, in his depth, complex and interesting.
Thus, each relationship is the beginning of discovery.
The excitement of achievement lies in pulling reality
out of dreams —
in looking back on the stepping-stone
that, from below, once looked like a barrier.

Joy is as available as progress; and
progress is as available as achievements and relationships.
Why don't we avail ourselves of more of all four?
Because they take effort!
Achievements require goals, plans, work, prayer.
Relationships require sacrifice, giving, effort, trials, courage.
Both involve risk.

Now, notice: reading over those requirements
is like reading over life's purposes.
We are here to know each other, to serve each other,
to build ourselves, to build others.
When we abdicate — when we take the easier road,
passing chances
for achievement and for relationships —
we fall prey to the regret implied in the words of Whittier:
"Of all sad words of tongue or pen,
The saddest are these: 'It might have been.' "

41

I challenge you to aim your life at worthy causes —
to say, as David did, "Is there not a cause." (1 Samuel 17:29.)

I challenge you to achieve —
to set clear objectives for five years,
for one year, for one month, for the coming week.

I challenge you to devote one disciplined hour to this process
every Sunday,
and to write your goals down —
to reflect on them, hone them, move always toward them.

I challenge you to live the "Noah Principle" —
to realize that there is a specific time when the rain will start,
to find your personal "ark" and *build* it!

I challenge you to value all the relationships you have —
to look for ways to know your family and friends better,
for ways to serve them,
for ways to deepen the ties.

I challenge you to form an expanding chain
of new relationships with
the kaleidoscope of brothers and sisters
that your life's current will carry you past.
I challenge you, while being not *of* the world,
to remain *in* the world — interested and involved
in many lives, many styles, many types of people,
seeking to find the good in them as well as to give
them the good in you.

I challenge you to learn to ask, to learn to listen,
to learn to "tune in" to another person's interests
(thus complementing him and benefiting yourself).

I challenge you to learn to look for good in people
until you *feel* praise and compliments for them.
Then I challenge you to give them that praise
and those compliments.

I challenge you to bridle and rein your life
hard into the fast and thrilling course
of planned achievement and caring relationships;
and as you do,

I Promise You That Your Mortal Relationships and Achievements Will "Carry Over" into Eternity

I promise you the quiet, inner fulfillment
(so much more important than public recognition)
of knowing you've done what you set out to do.
I promise you that love, that most important of all quantities/
qualities,
will grow in proportion to your life's relationships.

I Challenge You to Find the Full Joy of Understanding Life's Plan and Purpose

I had never enjoyed British football (soccer)
until one day when I sat by the coach.
(It's amazing what understanding can do for enjoyment.)

It is the same in the game of life.
We tend to love that which we understand
(we often *fear* that which we do not understand).

A simple and remarkably accurate definition of the gospel is
understanding.
The gospel is good news.
The good news is the *understanding* that God is our *Father*;
that there is both plan and purpose to life;
that the plan is agency, opposition, experience, and test;
that the purpose is joy.

The Lord's word yields understanding to those who study it —
but only a little understanding at a time,
only "line upon line."
Truths are often like dominoes, stood on end in line;
one falls and causes the next to fall.
One truth leads to another, and that to another.

As the truths come,
the bars fall away.
Truth makes us free (John 8:31-32);
freedom brings a higher, more open, clearer joy.

Knowledge comes to us as dew, distilling, but
the joy it brings comes to us like rain —
first a drop or two, then more, finally pelting down
in torrents, saturating us with the happiness
that God is our Father, that families are eternal,
that life has purpose, that everything counts.

The physical joys of body and earth
and the emotional joys of relationships and achievements
are heightened, intensified, expanded
by the mental-spiritual joys of understanding.

It's fun to drive a car,
but more fun if you understand how the car works.
It's a happy experience to be outdoors with nature;
but a happier one if you understand some of nature's workings,
and it's happier still if you realize that God made nature's
        beauties for you.
It's a joy to have a child,
but it brings more joy to know that the child came from a
        premortal existence,
and still more joy to know that the child can be yours forever.
And so on.

Understanding of truth brings freedom from doubt.
Understanding of laws brings freedom to do.

Understanding of God brings the freedom of faith.
Without understanding, there are no absolute values.
Without absolute values, "Why not?" becomes an answer
rather than a question.

I challenge you to gain understanding by study
of the ancient scriptures,
of the modern scriptures,
of the current scriptures given by today's apostles and
        prophets,
of the personal scripture of your patriarchal blessing.

I challenge you to gain understanding through
sweet prayer —
the kind of deep and personal dialogue that may go on
for more than just a few minutes,
and that includes listening and remembering
as well as talking.

I challenge you to gain understanding through advice
from those you respect and admire.
I challenge you to learn the fine art of advice-seeking;
to realize that even very important, very busy people
are flattered by a request for advice.

I challenge you to gain understanding through
sagacity — through close, interested observation
of the people and circumstances around you.

I challenge you to learn from the mistakes as well as from the
        successes
that you observe.

I challenge you, as you gain understanding,
to remember that *all* light and knowledge
comes from God.
I challenge you to let your understanding make you
more humble
as you appreciate the wideness of difference
between your understanding and His.

I challenge you to *look* for understanding;
and as you do,

I Promise You the Joy of Mortal Understanding
That "Carries Over" into Eternity

I promise you growing confidence, growing faith.
I promise you deeper relationships, more fulfilling
    achievements.
I promise you "sweet sorrow" rather than bitter.
I promise you more light,
which is the power as well as the insight of God.

I Challenge You to Find the Full Joy of Feeling God's Satisfaction

Brigham Young once asked a probing, frightening question:
"When you approach the throne of grace and petition the
      Father
in the name of the Savior who has redeemed the world, do
you use that name as the name of a stranger?"[1]

Ultimate joy is in knowing Christ, in feeling His personal love
and in feeling His satisfaction with our lives.
Each of the other "joys" is fragile.
Physical joy can be shattered by physical disaster.
Achievements can become failures, friends can change to
      enemies,
even understanding and faith can be undermined by doubt.
But *this* joy, the joy of having God's Spirit,
of His hand in your life,
and of feeling the pleasure of a real and loving Father,
cannot
be reversed
except through our own withdrawal from Him.

The joy of the Spirit reaches back and touches all other joys,
lighting them, intensifying them.

1. *Journal of Discourses* 7:274-5.

The Spirit sanctifies and renews our physical bodies (D&C
        84:33).
The Spirit enlightens and quickens our minds (D&C 11:13).
The Spirit "fine tunes" our sympathies, our emotions.
Medical science is increasingly convinced that chemicals
(their balance and imbalance)
substantially control our health, our receptivity, our ambition,
even our moods and personalities.
What most scientists do not know
is that spirit (our own and the Lord's) controls the chemicals.

As we draw close to God through righteousness,
we are touched by the Holy Ghost's influence.
As we receive God's covenants
we gain the more consistent gift of the Holy Ghost.
As we prove ourselves to ourselves, gaining charity,
expanding in hope and faith,
the gift becomes a Spirit of promise.
Then follows a Second Comforter,
then a sureness of calling and election
that can be mortality's ultimate joy—
that can, in fact,
move eternity's joy down
into the atmosphere of earth.

The influence of the Holy Ghost
brings the fruit of joy (see Galatians 5:22 and Romans 15:13).

The joy is not only manifest in comfort and peace;
it is also a joy of enthusiasm and excitement about life.
(Notice in Nephi's dream the enthusiasm of
the Holy Ghost as he invited Nephi to
"look"
and see the wonders and excitement of the earth's unfolding—
        1 Nephi 12:1.)

I challenge you to work to have the Spirit—
through obedience, through being anxiously engaged (D&C
        58:27),
through the "mental exertion" of faith. [2]

I challenge you to ask to have the Spirit—
(through "sweet prayer,"
through "crying to the Lord" as Enos did—Enos 1,
through humble "needing" of the Spirit in every effort).

I challenge you to use the priesthood often,
whether you hold it yourself or, as a wife, share it with your
        husband;
to officiate in the Lord's work;
to bless the sick;
to bless children and family members in times of dire need
and
in times of less critical need
(when they are particularly worried, when they face
a new challenge,
when you are going to be away from them for more than a
        day).

2. *Lectures on Faith 7:3.*

I challenge you to use the glorious principle of repentance—
often,
daily—
to clear your heart and soul of any offense,
small or large, and to cement
that repentance through the sacrament's commitment
each week.
As you seek the Spirit in these ways,

I Promise You Spiritual Joys That "Carry Over" into Eternity

I promise you a padlock, a safeguard on
all other joys of your life.
I promise you the highest level of joy—
joy that is deep and eternal.

**I Challenge You to Use One "Wish" to Get
"Ten More Wishes"**

Remember the smart second-grader?
You said, "What if you had just one wish?"
She said, "I'd wish for ten more wishes."

There may not be a wish that works like that,
but there is a
quality —
a quality which, if developed, gives you access
to ten more qualities,
or ten things,
or even ten wishes.

The quality is goal-setting and planning.
One who knows how,
and who does so within the framework of God's program,
can transform wishes into reality.

Our Heavenly Father designed earth to offer us two things:
1. A mortal journey of progress, growth, and achievement.
2. Joy along the way.

Thus, there are always two types of goals:
1. Goals that get us to the top of the mountain.
2. Goals that help us enjoy the climb.

Lack of attention to either type can derail a life.
The man whose only thought is the summit
misses the bird's song, the sunset,
the friendship of his fellow climbers;
he accepts the tragic trade of
achievements for relationships.
The man who loses sight of the peak
betrays his best self
and spends the night looking up at what might have been.

Generally,
I challenge you to set and meet
achievement goals and
relationship goals.

Specifically,
I challenge you to carefully, prayerfully
set five-year achievement goals, and
to break them down into one-year, one-month, and
one-week goals;
and to write out descriptions of the improved
relationships you desire.

More specifically,
I challenge you to spend a quiet, sober hour
early each Sunday morning
mentally working on your achievements

and relationships, following the pattern
of the books *Life Planning* and *Goals*,
or a pattern of your own design.

There is genuine excitement
in a goal met,
genuine power
in understanding the goal-striving process,
genuine joy in turning barriers into stepping-stones.
(Consider the joy of the eight-year-old who, after an hour
of study on ten hard spelling words, said,
"I know them, Dad.
I've turned those worries into happies.")

I challenge you to wish for more wishes —
to challenge yourself with
the pure oxygen of tuned, lofty goals,
to set them in your mind with repetition and commitment,
to pursue them with planning and persistence and
prayer;
and as you do,

and the joy of the journey — all along the way.
 · · · (your foreordination)

I Promise You the Joy of Reaching the Right Destination

I Challenge You to Undergo "Spiritual Conditioning" — Training of the Soul

I watch a parade each morning as I eat breakfast—
a parade of joggers,
conditioning their bodies.
It's a fad, a good fad, and many of the joggers
are marvelously consistent,
day after day, rain or shine, getting in those miles.

The earth is an object lesson;
physical comparisons teach us spiritual realities.
Conditioning the body should parallel
conditioning the spirit.
Let's try it.
Three things condition the body:
good eating, good sleeping, good exercising.
Now the spirit:
Good eating? Yes—we demand spiritual food, the scriptures;
we "feast upon the words of Christ" (2 Nephi 32:3).
Good sleeping? Yes—we rest in Christ's peace.
But what about the third one, the interesting one?
How do we exercise spiritually?
We look to some of the golden days of Zarahemla, the days
replete with joy and peace as Helaman reigned,
and there we find, in the "conditioning" language
of "stronger and stronger, firmer and firmer" (Helaman 3:35),

their growth in faith and humility.
What was their spiritual exercise?
"They did fast and pray oft. . . . ." (Helaman 3:35.)

Fasting is spiritual exercise. It
stretches the soul, stirs the spirit.

The physically unconditioned man never knows the joy
of a well-tuned body.
The spiritually unconditioned man
"receiveth not the things of the Spirit of God." (1 Corinthians
      2:14.)

As one conditions himself physically, he
becomes aware
of his particular physical gifts,
and he can concentrate on them
(quickness may cause him to focus on one sport,
strength on another, and so on).
As one conditions himself spiritually, he
becomes aware
of his particular spiritual gifts —
and all men have them (1 Corinthians 12:7-11) —
and he can concentrate on them.

Spiritual conditioning (scripture study, meditation,
fasting, prayer — all regular, all consistent)
can fill the body with light (D&C 88:67),
can make your body a living sacrifice (Romans 12:1),

and can bring faith, joy (Helaman 3:35),
and knowledge upon knowledge (D&C 42:61).

I challenge you to have a daily time for
scripture, meditation, and sweet prayer
(like physical conditioning, its effect
is cumulative, so consistency counts).
I challenge you to a partial fast *each* Sunday
(don't eat even the earliest breakfast until you have
talked with the Lord in a special Sabbath prayer).

I challenge you to set up a schedule for this conditioning—
to stay with it as rigorously
as you do your jogging schedule
or your schedule for going to work.

I challenge you to develop the discipline
to stay in spiritual training;
and as you do,

I Promise You the Joy of Knowledge Upon Knowledge

I promise you the joy of locating
a spiritual wellhead within your soul.
I promise you
that your heart's increased peace
and your soul's mounting joy
will be as obvious as strengthening muscle
on your arm.

I Challenge You to Make Decisions Before They Make You

A decision left to the wrong time, in the wrong place,
won't be made—it will make you.
Cases in point:
Bob, just married, still in school, pregnant wife,
small income, is trying to decide whether to pay tithing.

Jess, on the golf course with Larry, is trying to decide
whether to change jobs and move to Cleveland.

Kate, in love with a nonmember and listening
to him propose, is trying to decide if she should be
married in the temple.

Peggy, standing in the registration line, is trying
to decide what to major in at the university.

John, parked on an isolated road and heavily
involved emotionally and physically with his girlfriend,
is trying to decide if he should keep the law of chastity.

For Bob, Kate, and John, the timing is wrong,
and the odds are that the decisions they make
will be wrong.
Theirs are decisions of *law*,
and should thus have been firmly made in advance.
There is a *law* of tithing,

a *law* of celestial marriage,
a *law* of chastity.
Decisions of law should never be left to
the moment of crisis.
They can, and should, be made as early
as a person can understand commitment.

I challenge you to make your decisions of law
now
through the following process:
1. In your diary, make a list of all decisions
you are prepared to make *now*.
2. Write them as *commitments*, such as:
"I will go on a mission."
"I will live the Word of Wisdom."
"I will hold family home evening weekly."
You may list thirty or forty, or more.
3. Think yourself into the most difficult situation
you can imagine related to each commitment
on your list, and
commit *again* that you'll stick to it—
even then.
4. Sign and date the list—making it a binding contract
with yourself.

Jess and Peggy are in the wrong place,
doing the wrong thing to finalize their decisions.
Theirs are decisions of *faith*, and

they should be on their knees in a
"brother of Jared prayer"
(not, "How do we light our ships?"
but, "My decision is that these transparent stones will light our
        ships.
Will you touch them and confirm my decision?").

I challenge you to make your decisions of faith
through the process outlined in section 9 of the Doctrine and
        Covenants:
1.   Study the problem out carefully, prayerfully.
2.   Make your own best decision.
3.   Take that decision to the Lord for confirmation
(or for a "stupor of thought," which tells you
to start over).

I challenge you to make your decisions of law
now,
and to make your decisions of faith
according to the Lord's outline
and with His confirmation;
and as you do,

He has marked out for you.
the course
. . . and of knowing you are on

I Promise You the Joy of Being on the Lord's Side

One of the center-heart meanings of God's promise
that we can become like Him
is the glorious notion of eternal families.
He is a father, and He has the glory and pervasive peace
of a kingdom family,
with each of us as children.

The single factor that gives earth life its most overwhelming
            importance
is that it is here
where we, for the first time in eternity,
can begin kingdom-families of our own.

In all of eternity, our central roles will only change *once*:
from child to parent
(still child, but now also parent).

The deepest joys of earth come through families.
The deepest joys of eternity will also come
through families —
His and ours.

He invites us, here, to start eternal families;
and as we do,

I Challenge You to Find Yourself in Your Roots

Why do the scriptures place such emphasis
on genealogy?
on roots?
on knowing, genetically, from whence we came?
"Turn the hearts of the children to their fathers"
is one of the few phrases that is
repeated
in all major scriptural volumes
(see D&C 98:16, 110:15; Malachi 4:6; and 3 Nephi 25:6).
The tone is urgent:
"seek diligently to turn the hearts" (D&C 98:16),
"lest I come and smite the earth with a curse" (3 Nephi 25:6).
Why?
Wherein lies the importance?

The scriptures provide clues:
"the earth will be smitten with a curse unless there is a
welding link of some kind
between the fathers and the children" (D&C 128:18).

God's kingdom is a family.
His government is patriarchal.
Our families become kingdoms within His kingdom.
Thus, knowing our ancestors and doing things for them
forms the "links" of the government of God.

But it does more than that.
It helps us to know ourselves.
It gives us "rooted identities."

Common are the true stories about adopted children who
devote their mature lives
to finding out who their parents and ancestors are.
We *need* to know;
as we do, our own "link" ceases to
float in space.
It becomes, in our minds, part of a chain,
drawing strength and identity from
the links beyond.

As we come to know them, our ancestors
help us in many ways.
They show us where we got our gifts and traits.
They give us courage through their courage.
They give us faith through their faith.

I challenge you to know your roots,
not only by names and dates but by their journals,
by the times and places they lived,
by their families, by their jobs, by everything
you can learn about them.
I challenge you to put their pictures on your wall,
and on a family tree, so that your children
can see where they came from.

I challenge you to collect any experiences, any journals;
I challenge you to record on tape (or even videotape) the
        recollections
of any ancestors still alive —
and to preserve this record, and treasure it, and
pass it along.

I challenge you
to write your ancestors' experiences into
short stories for children,
and to use those stories with your own children
as bedtime stories.

I challenge you to do these
and any other things you can think of
to turn your hearts
to your fathers and to your roots;
and as you do,

I Promise You the "Kingdom Feeling" of Knowing Who You Are

I promise you joyful, righteous pride
in your name.
I promise you better understanding of your
own children.
I promise you deeper love of your
brothers and sisters.

I Challenge You to Give Joy to and Receive Joy from Your Children

Don't skip this chapter if you are not yet a parent.
Little children either are now or will someday be
your greatest stewardship.
If that time is not yet,
think of your little brothers and sisters,
or nieces and nephews,
or children who live in your neighborhood.
Be their friend,
learn from them,
prepare for your own.

When a child of God becomes a parent,
he undergoes the greatest role-change
of eternity.
He has always been a child;
and, through this great change — a change not of *degree*,
but of *kind* —
he becomes a parent.
He or she takes on a role which in one respect
is something like God's role —
father, mother.

The magnitude of the responsibility is awesome!
You become the parent
of one of
your eternal brothers or sisters.
There is no greater joy
than to raise children in truth,
to see them progress.

The Lord tells us that they are holy, these children,
and sanctified (D&C 74:7).
But He also warns that if you do not teach your children
the first principles of the gospel,
the sin will be upon your head (D&C 68:25).
In that case, grief will abound both on earth and in heaven.

So what do we do for our children?
Provide for them,
clothe them,
feed them.
Yes,
but what more?
Love them — deeply, unconditionally.
Yes,
but is that all?
Is love enough?
No, we must also teach them — at least the
first four principles of the gospel
(to avoid our own condemnation).

But what else must we teach them,
give them,
to maximize their progress?
to give them what God wants them to have?
to make them eternally happy?
to provide them with joy?

The last word of the question
is the answer.
We must give children the capacities for
joy
so that they will have what their Father
sent them here to gain (2 Nephi 2:25).

There are many kinds of joy.
The capacity for some joy is natural, already developed
in small children.
These joys must be preserved,
enhanced by parents.
Other joys must be learned by children,
with parents as the main teachers.

Here is a partial list:

Physical Joys
The joy of spontaneous delight (preserve)
The joy of the body (teach)
The joy of the earth (teach)

Mental Joys
The joy of interest and creativity (preserve)
The joy of imagination and creativity (teach)
The joy of order, goal-striving, and achievement (teach)

Social Joys
The joy of openness and candor (preserve)
The joy of communication and relationships (teach)
The joy of sharing and service (teach)

Emotional Joys
The joy of trust and the basic confidence to try (preserve)
The joy of uniqueness and self-assurance as an individual
    (teach)
The joy of security as part of a family (teach)

Spiritual Joys
The joy of basic faith (preserve)
The joy of decisions and obedience (teach)
The joy of spiritual insight and knowing God as a Father (teach)

The "preserve" joys can be preserved by
encouragement, confidence, praise, and by
learning *from* children, doing what they do.
The "teach" joys can be taught by
example,
by stories, games, and discussions,
and by whatever means you can develop.

I challenge you to provide well for your children.
I challenge you to love them unconditionally.
I challenge you to teach them
the first principles of the gospel
before their baptism.
I challenge you to give them the capacities
for joy.
I challenge you to raise them in light (D&C 93:40);
and as you do,

I Promise You the Kingdom Blessing
That Your Children's Joy Will Be Your Joy

I promise you that your good
will live eternally
through your children.
I promise you that each year of your life
will be happier than the last.

I Challenge You to Become a "Trunk" Between Your Roots and Your Branches

I sat one day beneath an enormous elm tree.
Its roots, big as my leg, were partly visible
and could be followed up through the corded trunk
and into the branches.
My mind focused on the trunk, nourished and buttressed by
the roots,
supporting and providing for
the branches.
I thought,
"I, along with my wife, am a 'trunk'
with roots and branches.
I am what's in between. I link one to the other.
Without me the roots dry up, the branches fall down.

"The roots represent the past, and carry in them
wisdom, knowledge, tradition,
and the joy of recall.
The branches are the future,
bright, sunlit, full of promise.

"I am the present — the tie between
past and future.
I can show the future branches to the past roots
and vice versa.

"I can be the conduit that helps them benefit
from each other.
I can plant in the branches the promises of the roots."
        (D&C 2:2.)

I began to comprehend, that day, why
the branches can't be perfect without the roots (D&C 128:5),
and vice versa.
I began to see that "perfect"
means "joy," and that "joy"
means "families."
Salvation is families, because the thing that is saved,
in the highest sense of that term,
is families.

It is trunks that make things one:
"I will gather together in one all things,
both which are in heaven [roots], and which are on earth
        [branches]." (D&C 27:13.)
And the earth thus avoids the curse (D&C 110:15; Malachi
        4:6),
because families linked together tend to be
better people.

I have a friend who, noting the likeness between his
eight-year-old boy and a boyhood photo
of his grandfather,
took his son to the old homestead of his grandfather,
dressed him in old-fashioned clothes,
and filmed him milking a cow and pumping water.
Later he brought his family together,
showed them a vision of grandfather as a boy,

and turned the hearts of children to their fathers.
He brought deep understanding, deep joy.

I challenge you to become a "trunk"—
to find ways to bring your extended family together,
to increase the "kingdom feeling" among them.

I challenge you to attend the temple often,
to think of the endowment in "kingdom" terms.
I challenge you to view the gospel itself
as the means of building kingdoms.
I challenge you to use the Church as a support vehicle for
     families (D&C 75:24),
to put family duties above all other duties (D&C 20:47).

I challenge you to set up family reunions,
family organizations,
to become the glue that fastens families fast;
and as you do,

I Promise You the Security of Being an Eternal Link in an Eternal Kingdom

I promise you the kingdom security
of being linked between strong roots and strong branches;
I promise you that, in your old age,
your children will be your crown (Proverbs 17:6).
I promise you that your family
will not be cursed at His coming.

I Challenge You to Make Your Family an Institution

Leo Tolstoy observed:

"Happy families are all alike; every
unhappy family is unhappy in its own way."[1]

One way in which happy families are similar
is in their institutionalization!
What is an institution?
It is a group of people, linked together
by tradition,
pride, objectives, modes, similar beliefs,
and (often) service.

A key virtue of institutions is that they provide
security and identity
for their members.
Good institutions do not sponsor uniformity and stereotype.
On the contrary, they provide the security base
that promotes confidence, individuality, uniqueness.

Great families are great institutions;
They are united in their commitment.
"As for me and my house, we will serve the Lord." (Joshua
       24:15.)
They are internally loyal and supportive.
"Teach them to love one another, and to serve one another."
       (Mosiah 4:15.)

1. *Anna Karenina.*

They are blessed and bonded by family prayer.
"Pray in your families." (3 Nephi 18:21.)
They are peaceful in their knowledge of truth.
"And all thy children shall be taught of the Lord,
and great shall be the peace of thy children." (3 Nephi 22:13.)

Great families are institutions because
they have traditions—
family "olympics" on July 24,
a family hike on the first day of spring,
a pumpkin-carving contest at Halloween,
help offered to a needy family on Thanksgiving,
a birthday cake for Jesus at Christmas.

Children who are part of institutionalized families
are secure, warm,
buffered
from the commotion and inconsistency of the world.
Parents of institutionalized families
share the same securities,
with the additional security
of feeling God's pleasure.

I challenge you to institutionalize your family
(whether your present role is parent *or* child).
I challenge you to have regularly scheduled things
that never change:
family prayer,
family home evening,

special family outings,
family secrets,
family goals.

I challenge you to buy a big, special book
and record in it
all family traditions, by month,
according to when they happen.
(One three-year-old became so oriented to
his family's traditions that he learned the months
not by name,
but by the family's tradition for that time of year—
"jack-o-lantern month,"
"picnic month," and so on.

I challenge you to have family projects.
(List them on a big board,
cross them off when your work together completes them.)
There are many possibilities:
learn a song together in a family orchestra,
prepare your house to be dedicated,
learn to play tennis together,
build a playhouse,
and so on.

The family that prays together stays together.
The family that works together stays together.
The family that plans together stays together.
Actually,

almost anything, done together,
keeps a family together.

I challenge you to make your family an institution,
and to realize that
families
are the *only* eternal institution on this earth;
and as you do,

I Promise You That Your Institution
Will Become a Kingdom

*I promise you that your children will
institutionalize their families,
which will add to your kingdom,
which will add to God's kingdom.*

I Challenge You to Have Individual Friendships with Each Family Member

You can't be personal friends with
a group.
People can only be friends with people.
Mormon sets the example for us by loving children with
a perfect love (Moroni 8:17).
Perfect love is individual love —
the kind of love that understands and empathizes,
and cares for each part of
a single, unique personality.

Children who are loved as individuals
become individuals,
with individual confidence, individual goals,
individual worth.

The larger a family is, the harder it is
to sustain individual relationships,
(and the more important it becomes).
Children, as they grow to adulthood,
will fall heir to the challenge to
"work out your own salvation" (Philippians 2:12).

To do this, they must know their own selves,
care about their own selves, respect their own selves.
This is much more possible for children
whose parents took the time to befriend them
as individuals.

Children who have individual friendships with
their parents
are less inclined to be intimidated or "put down"
when they see other peers who are better
at certain things than they are.
An individual friendship with a parent
gives them worth
and
heightens their awareness of their own particular gifts —
gifts that compensate for their lack of the
skill they are presently concerned about.

61

The other side of the coin is that you, as a parent,
will benefit. Every true friendship, whether the friend
is seven or seventy, is a learning experience,
a "lighting" experience.

If you don't have a family of your own yet,
apply the principle with each of your parents,
each of your brothers and sisters.
The rewards are happiness now,
for you and for them,
and expertise for you in doing the same thing
later
with your spouse
and your own children.

I challenge you to have a private "club"
with each of your small children,
according to their individual interests:
a model-building club with one,
a bike-riding club with another.

I challenge you to take each child on a "date"
regularly —
alone with you, away from the house,
perhaps letting the child choose where to go.

I challenge you to ask and listen
individually —
to use "Rogerian technique"
wherein you essentially repeat back what the child says
so the *child's* mind can determine the direction of the
        conversation.

I challenge you to have at least a moment of
private dialogue
with *each* child *each* day —
at bedtime, perhaps, or whenever you can,
but focusing *all* your attention
on *him*.
It's the complete attention, not the number of minutes, that
        matters.

I challenge you to have individual friendships
with each family member;
and as you do,

I Promise You a Kingdom of Joyful, Eternal Relationships

*I promise you that you will never lose the
confidence
of your children (Jacob 2:35).
I promise you that your children will become
"stripling warriors"
because of your teachings in their youth (Alma 56:47).*

I Challenge You to Establish a "Partnership of One"

We often think of the distinction of temple marriage
in *quantity* terms:
it lasts longer, it is bigger, it goes on forever.
The ideal way to view the everlasting covenant is
in *quality* terms:
because of its priesthood, its covenants, its sanctity,
it can be a purer union, a joyful contract,
and will
thus (and only thus)
be longer in quantity.

The highest level of exaltation
is reserved
for expanding kingdoms — for marriage partners
who are achieving oneness
with each other
and with their children (D&C 131:1-3).

Oneness
is the objective of marriage.
It is a synergistic oneness where the whole is greater
than the sum of its parts,
a oneness where the husband and wife are
joint heirs together (1 Peter 3:7),
a oneness where the man is not without the woman
nor the woman without the man in the Lord (1 Corinthians
        11:11).

Again, oneness does not mean loss of individuality,
oneness means one song,
where two separate strings, each with their own vibration,
harmonize
to create one composition.

The Lord's counsel is simple and absolute:
Husband, love your wife with all your heart (D&C 42:22),
even as you love your own body (Ephesians 5:28).
Provide for your family in spiritual and temporal ways.
Wife, submit yourself to your husband (Ephesians 5:22),
but be an equal partner in all things.
Be a joyful mother of children (Psalm 113:9).

Love within marriage is a signal flag of righteousness.
One of the few recorded instances when the
Lamanites were judged to be more righteous than the Nephites
was a result of husbands who loved their wives
and had not lost the confidence of their children (Jacob 2:35).

The oneness God sees for man and wife
is a glorious thing, with
each supported and strengthened and inspired by the other—
rejoicing together (Proverbs 5:18),
finding joy together (Ecclesiastes 9:9).

It is the oneness through which each partner
says to the other,
"With your love, all else in the world is bright."

I challenge you to create a partnership of one.
I challenge you to set goals and plan your weeks together—
perhaps in an "executive session" of family home evening,
after the children are in bed.
I challenge you to have private testimony meetings
at the close of those executive sessions.
I challenge you to plan your days together
the night before—while kneeling, before you have prayer.
I challenge you to pray together,
sometimes in the same prayer—one starting,
saying what he feels, stopping without an "amen,"
then the other concluding the same prayer.

I challenge you to continue your courtship
with a "date" each week—just you two, alone,
complete with opening doors and helping with the chair,
with little gifts, little notes, little looks.

I challenge you to make each other
your *top* priority—to *plan*
little ways to show your love.

I challenge you to sit and plan together regularly — to talk
about your children, to have
"five-facet reviews" in which you discuss
each child's physical, mental, social, emotional,
and spiritual status and growth.

I challenge you to do all this and more
to make your marriage
a partnership of one;
and as you do,

I Promise You an Eternally Expandable Kingdom

. . . a marriage of rejoicing and peace,
a flash of insight now
to heaven
and to godhood.

I Challenge You to Apply God's Parenthood and Christ's Sonship to Yours

As earlier stated,
we normally learn of the spiritual through the physical—
parables, object lessons, analogies with the *earthly*
help us to grasp the more difficult, but similar, *eternal*.

Here, the pattern is reversed.
We learn how to be successful earthly parents
by observing our perfect Heavenly Parent.
The principles He exhibits in dealing with us
(His children)
form the perfect pattern for our attempts in His role
(parenthood).

We note, in
viewing God's fathership, that:
1. He favors positive discipline
wherein our punishment consists of our not obtaining a
        reward,
rather than our being hurt or harmed.
2. He encourages His children to talk to Him often, and
to ask for their needs. He listens.
3. He requires us to seek our own answers, and
then to come to Him for confirmation
(rather than giving answers to us).
4. He gives us agency and freedom, but He teaches us

correct principles to govern ourselves, and He
is always there — not as a manager, but
as a consultant. Like a robin, He protects us
with His wing until we can fly, and then
He nudges us from His nest.
5.   He treats us and thinks of us individually,
not collectively.
6.   He is always calm.
7.   He is always consistent.
8.   He is always confident in us, offering encouragement.
(He praises the *try*, even without the result.)
9.   His goal — His work and His glory — is our
eternal happiness and well-being (Moses 1:39).
10.   He gives us laws and righteous tradition to
make our lives safe and secure.
11.   He loves us unconditionally.
12.   He is firm in His redress of our
wrong-doing, but He is always in control.

We learn equally great lessons from Christ's sonship:
1.   He was totally loyal to His Parent.
2.   He sought His Parent's counsel in all things.
3.   He asked His Parent for strength and confirmation,
but not for help without effort.

4. He respected His Parent and gave Him the credit.
5. He kept the laws ordained by His Parent.
6. He showed love for His Parent, and demonstrated constant gratitude and appreciation.

I challenge you to pattern both your parentship
and your sonship (or daughtership)
after God's.

I challenge you to develop a system of discipline
that centers on rewards
(perhaps a "star" for a child who does each thing on
"his list"
each day, a "black mark" for disobedience
or rule-breaking,
a reward at the end of the week for each star
and each day with no black mark).
I challenge you
to incorporate
each of the listed twelve fatherhood traits of God
into your parenthood —
consciously, strategically; *plan* them in.

I challenge you to teach your children
about Christ —
that He is the source of their forgiveness (2 Nephi 25:26).
I challenge you
to "labor diligently" to help your children
"believe in Christ" (2 Nephi 25:23).

I challenge you to pray for your children as
powerfully as Alma did for his (Mosiah 27:14).
I challenge you, whether or not you are a parent,
to be the kind of son (or daughter)
that Christ was —
loyal, loving, responsible.

I challenge you to take as your model
in your ultimate stewardship of the family
the ultimate models — God and Christ;
and as you do,

**I Promise You That Your Kingdom
Will Begin to Liken Itself to His**

I promise you that your children
will respect you as well as love you.
I promise you that God, the ultimately advanced father,
will bless your beginning parenthood.

POSTSCRIPT: I Challenge You to Remember

Have you ever forgotten a promise
or a commitment
or a resolution you made?
A key difference between God and man is that
we forget
often.

Perhaps the same veil that blocks our immortal memory
impedes our mortal one.

If we could only remember what we decide to do
long enough to do it!
(This last year, my New Year's resolution
was to remember the resolution from the year before.)

I challenge you to employ two ways
of remembering
the challenges of this book
(so that you will not lose the promises).

1.   *Repetition*
Work on one challenge per week
(the twenty-one challenges this book contains will take
        twenty-one weeks).
Then start over again (on week twenty-two) with challenge
        number one.
You will then "use" the book three times during the year,
remembering the challenges (and remembering to *do* them)
a little better each time.

2. *Written commitment*
When you decide to accept a challenge,
write your commitment in your journal.
Then form the habit of looking back through your journal
regularly.

View commitments as promises to the Lord.

I challenge you to remember these promises to the Lord;
and as you do,

I6

6

BEGINNINGS

by CAROL LYNN PEARSON

Illustrated by Trevor Southey

Doubleday & Company, Inc.
Garden City, New York

PREFACE

*And when he was entered into a ship . . .
there arose a great tempest . . . And his dis-
ciples came to him, and awoke him, saying,
Lord, save us: we perish. And he saith unto
them, Why are ye fearful, O ye of little faith?
Then he arose, and rebuked the winds and the
sea; and there was a great calm.*

(St. Matthew 8:23-26)

There are so many storms in life. It is often difficult to
find solutions to our problems. Some of us despair. Others
seek an escape. Those who follow these paths, however, have
never fully realized that life was meant to be a challenge
and an opportunity.

The challenge lies in being able to choose between dif-
ferent types of satisfactions. Wisdom lies in being able to
choose the diamond instead of its glass imitation.

The opportunity consists in learning from one's experience.

*If thou art called to pass through tribulation
. . . if fierce winds become thine enemy; if the
heavens gather blackness, and all the elements
combine to hedge up the way . . . know thou, my
son, that all these things shall give thee experience, and shall be for thy good. The Son
of Man hath descended below them all. Art thou
greater than he?*

(Doctrine and Covenants 122:6-8)

Among the great Gifts He offers to us are the Principles
which He knew must be understood, accepted and lived if
we are to attain the destiny forseen for each of us from the
Beginning of Beginnings.

*Behold, I am Jesus Christ . . . In me shall all
mankind have light, and that eternally, even
they who believe on my name; and they shall
become my sons and my daughters.*

(Ether 3:14)

Carol Lynn understands these Principles. In humility
and with integrity she has explored Their deep and delicate
meanings.

All of us who read her poems (and may there be many
of us) can best express our gratitude to Him and to her by
seeking with all our hearts and souls to "become" His Son
or Daughter. Then we will find Peace and Joy as He understood them. We can sleep when the wind blows.

Reed H. Bradford

CONTENTS

BEGINNINGS

Today
You came running
With a small specked egg
Warm in your hand.
You could barely understand,
I know,
As I told you
Of Beginnings —
Of egg and bird
Told, too,
That years ago
You began,
Smaller than sight.
And then,
As egg yearns for sky
And seed
Stretches to tree,
You became —
Like me.

Oh,
But there's
So much more.
You and I,
Child,
Have just begun.

Think:
Worlds from now
What might we be? —
We,
Who are seed
Of Diety.

ANALYSIS

I am,
They announce
Authoritatively,
A product of
Environment
And heredity.

True.
But my substance
Is laced with
One thing more:
Thin threads of
The now-forgotten
Everything
That I was
Before.

RITUAL

Why ritual?
May I not receive
Christ without burial
By water?
If I remember
That He bled,
If I believe,
What need for
Sacramental bread?

Only this I know:
All cries out
For form —
No impulse
Can rest
Until somehow
It is manifest.
Even my spirit,
Housed in heaven,
Was not content
Until it won
Embodiment.

OF THE MYSTERIES

I know only as much of God and the world
As a creature with two eyes must;
But what I do understand I love,
And what I don't understand, I trust.

THE ELEVENTH HOUR

Had I been born
To other centuries —
How pleasant
To stretch
In the sun
And choose from
All life's
Possibilities
This one,
Or that.
To prove the
Earth is round,
Or tame the ocean,
To write a dictionary,
Or expound
On Shakespeare's
Subtle irony.

But these are
Daytime jobs.
And,
As I was born
To time's
Saturday night,
My ordained task
Is to kindle
The Sabbath light.

FROM A WRITER
OF PLEASANT THINGS

You must forgive
This tendency of mine
To believe
The world holds
Something good,
Something fine.

The habit
Has troubled me
From childhood —
When I even
Preferred to
Build a snowman
Than to take
A romp through
The garbage can.

THE LORD SPEAKS TO A
LITERARY DEBAUCHÉ
NEWLY ARRIVED IN HEAVEN

Impressive indeed, this shelf of books
On which all the earth-critics dote.
But oh, my son, how I wish that you
Had read the book I wrote.

MILK BEFORE MEAT

Why worry on
Exactly how
A body will arise
Once a man dies?

I can't even
Understand
The manifest things —
Like how
A seagull flies
From merely
Having wings.

PERSPECTIVE FROM MORTALITY

My life is patterned as the palm
Of a rain-washed leaf, calm,
Cut, and full.
But
I view my life from underneath,
Which — like the patterned leaf —
Is fuzzed and dull.

A NEW DIMENSION TO FAITH

When some new pain pierces my life
Rebellion begins to cry,
"God knew this would come and He approved!"
But wait, long ago—so did I.

KEEPING THE BUCK

I can't blame God for what I am,
Nor for the troubles that surround me:
He did His best with what I was
When He found me.

THE PLAN

An unseemly design for ascension,
That with a cross and a crown of briar
We should lift Christ toward heaven
So that He could lift us higher.

TO A BELOVED SKEPTIC

I cannot talk with you of God
Since sober wise you grew;
So my one recourse in charity
Is to talk with God of you.

THE LESSON

Yes, my fretting,
Frowning child,
I could cross
The room to you
More easily.
But I've already
Learned to walk,
So I make you
Come to me.

Let go now —
There!
You see?

Oh, remember
This simple lesson,
Child,
And when
In later years
You cry out
With tight fists
And tears —
"Oh, help me,
God — please." —
Just listen
And you'll hear
A silent voice:

"I would, child,
I would.
But it's you,
Not I,
Who needs to try
Godhood."

NATIVITY SCENE

Touch the tiny Jesus gently now —
Put him in the bed.
No, dear, I don't know why the wise man
Wears a turban on his head.
That's just the way they dressed.
Be careful with the lamb—it's best
To hold him with both hands.
It's late in Bethlehem —
That's why the star shines bright.
It showed the wise men where to come.

No, dear, the star can't really shine.
It's wood—it's just pretend.
But last night,
The star we wished on high above the moon —
That was real. Remember?

The lamb won't bleat, dear.
Even when you're asleep.
It's a sort of clay. But you did hear
Your uncle's sheep
Calling in alarm
Through the midnight of a snow-filled farm.

The baby Jesus?
Clay.
But listen, dear (put down the lamb) —
I've a promise for you,
A promise God will keep:
As you've seen stars
And as you've heard the sheep,
One day you'll know and hear and see
This Jesus too,
In reality.

THE BENEFICIARY

I was not there.
But they say
It happened for me.
On the cross it happened,
And in the tomb.
For me —
Vicariously.

But how?
It was His sacrifice
Not mine.
It was He who wept,
Who bled,
Not me.

Except —
Why, look —
At the flick of a finger
I instantly receive
What Edison
Gave his full life
To achieve.

Perhaps,
If one man,
Searching the skies,
Willed us the key
To conquer night —
May not another,
A greater,
Bequeath from the cross
The key to
Eternal light?

THOUGHTS
IN THE CHAPEL

How I will
Greet the Lord
In heaven
I do not know.

But here
With the
Sabbath organ
And water and bread,
Or at home
Beside my bed —
Whenever we converse,
Just Him and me
(Watching the sunset
Or the sea),
I can at least
Rehearse.

TO ONE WHO WORRIES
ABOUT BEING FOUND

Does the flower fret
That the bee
Might forget
To buzz by?

Ah, no.
One concern
Has she,
And she tends
It well:
Her own smell.

THE EMBRYO

Love is no eagle,
Strong amid
The heights.
It is an egg —
A fertile,
Fragile
Possibility.
Hold it warm
Within your wing,
Beneath your breast.

Perhaps in heaven
Love can live
Self-nourished,
Free.
But in this world,
Where mountains fall
And east winds blow,
Oh, careful —
Love is embryo.

MY SEASON

Seeing the tree
Beneath a baptism of snow,
You may call her barren.
But is it so?
And for all your watchings
On a March night
When the twigs seem dark
And the bark
Feels cold to your hand —
Can you call her fruitless
And so leave?

She smiles,
Calm in the station
Of seasons
And in the ordination
Of sun, and sap, and spring.

As for me?
You turn away,
Impatient with
The promises you've seen.
But—inside I fill
And pulse and flow
With the urgency of green.

I've a season,
Like the tree.
And all your
Faithless doubts
Will not destroy
The rising spring
In me.

ANOTHER BIRTH

I did not bring
The anticipation
Of birth —
Of forging my spirit
With flesh.

As the moment
Neared,
I think
I held my breath
(If spirits breathe)
And made a
Reverent plunge
Into embodiment,
Mortality.

Yes —
Even unremembering
I know the
Wonderment,
The awe.
For I stand staring
At another birth
That swells my heart
With the hugeness
Of beginnings.
In a moment
I am born as wife —
Given another body
And another life.

AT THE ALTAR

The thought
Of forever
Teased my mind
Like a mountain
Through a thickly
Misted view.

But today the
Veil dissolved
To show —
Eternity
Is you.

A JUDGMENT

I have been judged.
Already, mortal,
I have stood
At heaven's bar
While my soul
Was read aloud.
And —
Oh, listen —
Not proud,
But too full
For silence
I sing the decree.
God smiled at me
(And all of
Heaven did too),
Smiled as He gave
A sentence
Toward salvation —
Gave me you.

THE REASON

A certain panic
Finds me
When I see
A forest, a train,
A library.
So many trees to touch,
Places,
Faces yet to view,
And, too,
So many words to read.

If I concede
All space to earth,
All time to life,
The disproportion
Is absurd
(My tiny taste
And the giant waste
Of all creation
I've not known).
What a wretched,
Faithless view
Of God's economy.

It isn't true.
The forest, the train,
The library —
Are why we have
Eternity.

PRAYER AT TABLE

The food, yes —
But most of all
Bless
Me.
The bread is
Full and good,
As I would be.
Oh, Lord,
My only leaven,
Work —
Warm me —
Let me lift
Toward heaven.

GUILT

I have no vulture sins, God,
That overhang my sky,
To climb, grey-feathering the air,
And swoop carnivorously.

It's just the tiny sins, God,
That from memory appear
Like tedious, buzzing flies to dart
Like static through my prayer.

AUTHORITY

There is
A fire that filters
Down the night
Of this world—
A light-line
Sparked by God
In human lanterns.
I watch them
And my way clears.

But here
One flickers,
Then fails,
And farther off
Another's glow
Guides only the
Largest steps.

Still I can see.
For God also kindled
(And gently blows
To brighten)
A flame
In me.

PURIFICATION

If the sea
And the sun
Can bleach a bone
Til it's whiter
Than a gull,
Cleaner than foam —

Oh, how bright
My soul
Can emerge,
Purged
On the beach
Of Christ's water
And light.

And —

How calm
And warm
His sand.

THE FORGIVING

Forgive?
Will I forgive,
You cry.
But
What is the gift,
The favor?

You would lift
Me from
My poor place
To stand beside
The Savior.
You would have
Me see with
His eyes,
Smile,
And with Him
Reach out to
Salve
A sorrowing heart —
For one small
Moment
To share in
Christ's great art.

Will I forgive,
You cry.
Oh,
May I —
May I?

PROPERTY

Collect property?
The road to the
New Jerusalem
Will seem hard
To those with
A fortune
To discard.

Just one lovely thing
That I may
Reverently bear
To the City of God
(A silver plate
Or perhaps a ring) —
This,
With the greater
Wealth locked lightly
In my breast,
Is all the estate
I care
To accumulate.

THE TITHE

Into the crockery
Of a crumbling earth
I pour my
Nine-tenth's wealth.
But how the
Remaining coin
Cheers my economy,
As it clinks
In the golden cup
Of eternity.

THE MEASURE

Friend,
Do you measure land
With a barometer?
Can you understand
The law of gravity
By testing
The freezing point of mud
At its greatest density?

There is no God
By knowledge's rules?
Friend,
Examine your tools.

To discover God
You must form your plan
To the nature
Of God Himself,
Not the nature of man.
The only key
Is that forgotten faculty
That pulses through you
Now and then,
Eluding the hand
And startling the mind.
Spirit, it's called.

Friend,
You will not find
God through mistaken tools.
Who weighs a stone
With a measuring tape?
Fools.

PRAYER

This radio set
Called prayer
Is designed
For remarkably
Simple repair.
When the lines fail,
There is no doubt
Which half
Of the set
Is out.

THE OFFERING

For ancient wrongs
God required
The burning of flesh,
An offering fresh
From the flocks.

But Christ turned
The outside in.
And for my sin
God demands
The harder part:
No yearling lamb
On the altar,
But my own
Wounded heart.

THE PRICE

Anguish, yes,
But not despair.

This agony that
Ties your breath
Is a law
The fruitful
Must bear.

Ask the
Almost-mother,
Her body
Heaving and torn —
Only from
Exquisite pain
Is beauty born.

DAY-OLD CHILD

My day-old child lay in my arms.
With my lips against his ear
I whispered strongly, "How I wish —
I wish that you could hear;

"I've a hundred wonderful things to say
(A tiny cough and a nod),
Hurry, hurry, hurry and grow
So I can tell you about God."

My day-old baby's mouth was still
And my words only tickled his ear.
But a kind of a light passed through his eyes,
And I saw this thought appear:

"How I wish I had a voice and words;
I've a hundred things to say.
Before I forget I'd tell you of God —
I left Him yesterday."

INVESTMENT

How enviously
I watched
The rose bush
Bear her bud —
Such an easy,
Lovely birth.
And
At that moment
I wished
The sweet myth
Were true —
That I could
Pluck you,
My child,
From some
Green vine.

But now
As you breathe,
Through flesh
That was mine
(Gently in the
Small circle
Of my arms),
I see
The wisdom
Of investment.

The easy gift
Is easy to forget.
But what is bought
With coin of pain—
Is dearly kept.

FROM A WOMAN

Is it, then,
That the trunk
Of the tree
Is man,
And the branch
Is me?

Oh, look—
How high
The leaves lean
To the sky,
And the springtime
Blossoms burst
To beauty,
Then to fruit.

Is there
A wish more worthy
Than to be
A bearer of harvests
Eternally?

GOD SPEAKS
TO ABRAHAM

Why
The almost-sacrifice?
Why the knife
Above your only son
While you wept?

Oh, Abraham,
I needed one
Who could understand.
There will be
Another lifted
On the hill
Of sacrifice.
And another
Father will watch,
Will weep.

But no
Merciful angel,
No man,
Oh, none
Shall stay
Death's hand
To save
My son.

TO MY ANCESTORS

I wonder—
Did I peek
Through the veil
Impatiently,
While you slowly
Forged
The bonds that
Brought me to
Mortality?

And
Do you now stand
Where I stood
Yesterday,
Your cheeks against
Heaven's curtain,
And pray—
Pray fervently
For me to forge
The bonds that
Bring us to
Eternity?

FULL CIRCLE

I shall close the circle, Grandmother,
Whose first half brought
You to these mountains.

On eight-year-steady legs you walked
Beside the wagon, brushing the dust
From your mouth with hands that
In the night reached out for
The dolls you left in Nottingham.
Your wide eyes watched the wooden
Coffin close over your sister Lucy,
A mother's tear frozen on her still face.
Fourteen hundred miles of strange night noises
And the hurt of hunger
And feet that cried for rest.
"But where are we going, Mother?"
"To Zion, dear. Hold the blanket tight."
"Mother, what is Zion?"
"Zion is the pure in heart.   Sleep."

Did you know, Grandmother,
As you laid your daughter in a cradle
That she would lay a daughter in a cradle
Who would close the circle?
This bit of lace you brought from
Over the sea will be in my pocket.
And I will pray that you are there
Among the hosts that go before,
Keeping the pillar of fire.

I may have a child who cries out in the night
For his own bed in the valley of the Wasatch.
He won't understand why there are no trains
To travel the fourteen hundred miles.
He may turn to me as we lie on the prairie floor.
"But where are we going, Mother?"
"To build the New Jerusalem.
Hold the blanket tight."
"But why are we going, Mother?"
"Because Christ is there."

Our circle, Grandmother,
And Adam's larger circle, too:
Eden of old,
Jerusalem anew.

TO THE CHRISTIAN
NOW BLESSED WITH
ROSES INSTEAD OF
TAR AND FEATHERS

Remember Aesop's
Tale of the
Traveler?
Please note:
The wind failed
To make him
Shed his coat.
It was the sun
That won.

MONTHLY FAST

One foodless day—
An inspired control:
Good rest
For my body,
Good exercise
For my soul.

WATER AND SPIRIT

My birth today
Is substance of
Heaven's true poetry:

Baptized into
Christ's burial—
God's perfect simile.

THE WATCHERS

There is a tomb
In old Jerusalem
Where one is told
Christ spent
Death's interim.
And many walk
That way
In curiosity.

"Three days
Behind the stone,"
He said,
"And then
A longer time
In heaven before
I come again."

But few
There are
Who watch
That door.

PROVISION FOR THE END

What to do when
The dawn brings night
And the moon spins out
And the stars fall white?

Wait calm in the silence
The black sky spilled:
Your lamp will light—
If it is filled.

JUDGED

I don't fret
As to where
My soul will
Be assigned—
Whether I'll find
Me with the Celestial
Or not quite
Qualify.

It's simple:
Water meets
It's own level—
So shall I.

EARTH-SOUL

The earth
Has a soul—
I know.
How else came
The sorry groans
That heaved
A rush of
Fire and wind
And blood and
Crashing stones?

She felt the
Sad procession
Climb the hill—
She heard
The nails—
She knew.
And with the
Bursting
Of the heart
Upon the cross,
Her heart burst
Too.

GOD SPEAKS

Death is ugly?
Oh, my children,
No.

If you knew
The beauty
That begins where
Your sight fails,
You would run,
Run, run,
And leap
With open arms
Into eternity.

But sad
Is a harvest
Of green wheat.

And,
So you would
Feverishly
Cling to earth
And finish
Your mortal task,
I merely gave
Death
An ugly mask.

OF PLACES FAR

To me Istanbul
Was only a name,
Until a picture
You took
Of the Blue Mosque
Came.

I don't receive
Postcards from heaven
Showing Saint Peter
At prayer,
But, oh—that place
Is real enough,
Now that
You are there.

BOUND

There's something strangely false in our
Assured, complete goodbye,
For love's the blood in the flesh of the soul
And the soul will never die.

So—friendly, fondly, as I may
In God's approving view,
I'll call across eternity
For messages of you.

WOMAN-CHILD

As a child
I saw her hand
(That had guided
My mouth to her breast)
Posed carefully
To rest
Upon a pleated robe.
Unwillingly
It froze.

Will she mind,
I wonder,
That when next we meet
She will not find
A small brown head
For her fingers
To caress,
But instead
A woman-child
In woman's dress?

MEMORIAL

This rose I give
To your grave
Is lovely, yes,
But I must confess
A little shame
To place these petals
Beside your name.

Tomorrow the rose
Is brown and dead,
Now bright and vernal.
But, oh—
Your season
Is eternal.

POINT OF VIEW

Sun and mountain meet.
"Look," I say.
"Sunset!"

But I forget
That far away
An islander
Wipes morning
From his eyes
And watches
The same sun
Rise.

What's birth?
And death?
What's near
Or far?
It all depends
On where you are.

DEATH

Death is the great forget, they said,
A mindless, restful leaving
Of all consciousness and care
In a vast unweaving.

And so I waited, cramped and still,
For approaching Death to bring
Forgetfulness—but all he brought
Was a huge remembering.

MEMENTOS
OF MORTALITY

I do not write
That my words
Might save
Some small
Piece of me
Beyond the grave.
Oh, I shall
Be quick long
Past the day
The last reader
Has put the
Book away.
And with use
Fulfilled,
These words
I write shall be
Happy mementos
Of mortality.